THE PLANT
AND THE TREE

THE PLANT
AND THE TREE

Published by Krystal Lee Enterprises (KLE Publishing) Copyright © 2025 by K. Lee
All rights reserved.
Please send comments and questions:
Krystal Lee Enterprises
services@KLEPub.com
sales@KLEPub.com

To Reach the Author:
Email: me@authorklee.com me@drkrystallee.com
Web: AuthorKLee.com Social Media: @AuthorKLee 770-240-0089 Ext. 1

ISBN: 978-1-945066-89-4

Dedication

This book is dedicated to my mother, who believes in family, teaching, and training up a child in the way that they should go. I love you, Yulanda, aka, Punkin!

To my siblings and children, cousins, and extended family, hugs.

To the readers of this book, may you enjoy the powerful message of how we all start off like seeds and grow into plants and trees.

To the Father, who gives me the ability to write and do all that I do, thank you!

There were young children playing with their grandmother affectionately known as "Punkin." She got the nickname, I think, because her eyes are hazel brown and glistened in the sunlight. Her eyes from the time of her youth had a glow that no one knew would shine into her old age.

She kept a happy face and was patient and kind. This doesn't mean she wouldn't hand out a spanking or two when her grandchildren overstep the line. She helped them out by saying, "Now, you need a spanking, then you will be just fine."

She did believe in discipline and never apologized for it, but more than she believed in discipline, she believed in teaching. She was never shy about teaching her grandchildren how she did the things she does. One of the things she loved and was very good at was plants.

You could go into her house, and you would see at least 10 potted plants. On her front porch, she spread the love there, too. Some of her plants were growing with vegetables or fruits. She would stick some of everything into the dirt, and today, a group of her grandchildren saw her working with her plants, and they had questions.

One of her grandchildren asked, "Grandma Punkin, what you doing?" With a warm smile, she replied, "I am taking care of my plants."

Another grandchild says, "Grandma, can we watch you with your plants?"

Don't be afraid to invite your children into the things you do. To be patient and kind when they ask, even if that means slowing down. Don't trouble the little ones to learn the Good News.

Grandma Punkin had a lot to do before the rain fell, but she wanted to nurture the interest in her grandchildren. So she began to explain. I am repotting some of my plants because they are outgrowing their location. Every plant has a size, a habitat, and a living condition it likes."

"Some like full sun, and others like to be in the shadows. Some want a lot of water, and others very little." They both want and need different things to live, and for the leaves not to turn brown."

"Oh, okay, so you are changing the pots. So do you just pour the dirt from one pot to the next?"

"Sometimes, but you usually have to add more dirt because what the plant had before is not likely enough in a new pot. Some plants like a lot of dirt, and others, not so much. So you have to learn what the plant needs. I have spent years working with plants, and they don't start off like this."

"Wait, they don't come like this?"

"You can buy a plant already nurtured by someone else, but all plants come from seeds or a bud."

"How can something so large come from something so small?"

"You are like a plant. When you were first thought of and formed in your mother's stomach. You were a seed. You were a tiny organism with life waiting to be fertilized and nurtured in the womb."

"The womb?"

"Yes, silly, the womb. That is another word for the part of a woman's stomach where babies can grow. Here you spent about 9 months growing from an embryo, a tiny baby, and a seed, to a large seed. Some fruits, like the mango, have a large casing that covers the seed inside. You don't plant that, but the seed within the shell."

"Wow, so I am like a mango?"
They all start to laugh.

"Like a mango, as you grow, you
go from this small fruit to being
able to plant a tree!"

"A tree, Grandma? That is really
big!"

"Plants and seeds have the ability to bear fruit of all sizes. No matter how big the person or animal, they all need or consume something that started off with a seed. Yah, God, knows how to use the small things to confound the wise. We may think that the little things don't matter, that children or seeds don't matter, but they all do!"

Genesis 1:28-31

28 And God blessed them. And Yah said to them, "Be fruitful and multiply and fill the earth and subdue it, and have dominion over the fish of the sea and over the birds of the heavens and over every living thing that moves on the earth." 29 And Yah said, "Behold, I have given you every plant yielding seed that is on the face of all the earth, and every tree with seed in its fruit. You shall have them for food. 30 And to every beast of the earth and to every bird of the heavens and to everything that creeps on the earth, everything that has the breath of life, I have given every green plant for food." And it was so. 31 And God saw everything that he had made, and behold, it was very good. And there was evening and there was morning, the sixth day.

"What else, Grandma, should we know about a seed?"

"A seed needs light, water, and food to grow. Sometimes the things we think that stink and have no value are the things that a seed needs to grow. Cow manure is one of the best fertilizers, because the waste from a cow is filled with nutrients the cow ate. The cow doesn't have to be perfect in all the things it does for the Good Lord to decide to use its waste to bless something else."

"So what are you saying, Grandma?"

"That your parents are meant to help you grow from the positive things they do, and even their mistakes can help you grow."

"The Father is able to teach each of us how to love and be loving when we have imperfect people who He can use to give you what you need to grow."

Luke 8:9-15

9 And when his disciples asked him what this parable meant, 10 he said, "To you it has been given to know the secrets of the kingdom of God, but for others they are in parables, so that 'seeing they may not see, and hearing they may not understand.' 11 Now the parable is this: The seed is the word of God. 12 The ones along the path are those who have heard; then the devil comes and takes away the word from their hearts, so that they may not believe and be saved.

Luke 8:13-15

13 And the ones on the rock are those who, when they hear the word, receive it with joy. But these have no root; they believe for a while, and in time of testing fall away. 14 And as for what fell among the thorns, they are those who hear, but as they go on their way they are choked by the cares and riches and pleasures of life, and their fruit does not mature. 15 As for that in the good soil, they are those who, hearing the word, hold it fast in an honest and good heart, and bear fruit with patience.

30

"Everyone has a seed, a purpose for why they were put on earth. If we are patient and give ourselves what we need to develop and grow, someday, any seed will mature into a plant or a tree that can help others. We can be a guide to those who will someday need us."

"In the same way I am spending time and explaining to you about plants, seeds, growth, and life, you too should spend time with someone doing the same thing. This is what is meant by a word being a seed."

"An encouraging word to someone or an explanation for how something works can help someone else grow in ways you won't always be able to quickly see. When you first water a plant, you don't see how it is growing. Don't be discouraged. If you give it time, and keep providing it with a good environment, one filled with nutrients, love, and discipline, the seed will grow!"

"This is how a seed turns into a tree, by slowly progressing and not getting upset with the journey."

"Grandma, are we still talking about plants?"

"You know I had to use my preaching hat to help ya'll out a little bit more. But a short description of how a plant grows is like this:"

"A seed is planted, and the seed likely came from a full-grown plant or tree."

"The plant's offspring, then, is planted in good soil. Not soil in opposition of its growth. The plant is getting the right amount of sunlight, water, care, and attention."

"As the plant grows, you may see only dirt in the beginning. But if you are patient, it will start to bud. You will see a green stem shoot up from the dirt. Then it will start to grow leaves."

"If it is a plant, it will bloom its flowers after the leaves form. For perennials, flowers that grow and die off temporarily after they bloom, they come back again next year! So they keep on growing but go dormant under the earth for a season."

"For annual plants, they only bloom once, and you will have to go get more seeds to keep producing the plant."

"For the plants that grow into a tree, they take longer to mature than a few months or years. Like how you children take nearly twenty years to become a tender tree. At 20 years old, you still have a whole lot of living to do to mature and grow as big as an oak tree. Do you know that some oak trees can live for 900 and even 1,000 years?"

"Wow, that's old!" says one of her granddaughters.

"We don't live that long like Methuselah in the Bible, but the blessed can live to be over a hundred years old! Did you know that many members of our family lived to be 97? Harriet Tubman lived to be 91 and saw the transformation of our people going from slaves to freedom! A lot can happen in 100 years with little seeds that are strong enough to believe in big dreams!

"Before you can appreciate the trees you see, you must marvel at what brought the tree. Little seeds are the beginning of life. We shouldn't despise the humble beginnings we all have, thinking they won't amount to anything. Nor should we assume because the family we came from, wasn't a good example, we have no hope for a good life."

"In the Father's hands, He can make anyone's life and dreams complete! Be a seed who aspires to be as timeless as an oak tree. Share words that help to build up others, long past your years. The gift of a seed is small, but the smallest seed, a Mustard Seed, can grow to produce the largest tree!"

Matthew 13:31-32

31 He put another parable before them, saying, "The kingdom of heaven is like a grain of mustard seed that a man took and sowed in his field. 32 It is the smallest of all seeds, but when it has grown, it is larger than all the garden plants and becomes a tree, so that the birds of the air come and make nests in its branches."

When you allow your seed to grow, no matter how many years you live, you become a perennial plant, even a tree that grows so large, birds can come and rest in your branches.

You become a book that people can read. A piece of technology that sticks in culture, or bring the gift of healing when you become a nurse.

You protect the innocent when you become a police officer. You become a gift of good news when you preach. You become a guiding light when you parent and grandparent. We are growing from seeds to plants, and our legacy is the tree!"

Galatians 6: 9-10

6 Let the one who is taught the word share all good things with the one who teaches. 7 Do not be deceived: Yah is not mocked, for whatever one sows, that will he also reap. 8 For the one who sows to his own flesh will from the flesh reap corruption, but the one who sows to the Spirit will from the Spirit reap eternal life. 9 And let us not grow weary of doing good, for in due season we will reap, if we do not give up. 10 So then, as we have opportunity, let us do good to everyone, and especially to those who are of the household of faith.

Believe in family, preserve your legacy. Tell your *story*. Make your journey as strong as a tree.

Dr. Lee has authored over forty-five books across more than twelve genres: adult, children, youth fiction, self-help, spiritual growth, comedy, novels, business, empowerment and more to help people in their most profound times of need.

She is also passionate about coaching programs WAE Process (Write Anything Easily), Embrace Your Crown, Turn Key Solution for Small and New Businesses, and The Lesson for Youth and Teenagers.

- Connect with me using the QR or visit
- AuthorKLee.com
- Social sites with the handle: AuthorKLee

Shop books by Author K. Lee

Explore my author catalog and discover the wide range of books I have available for the whole family!

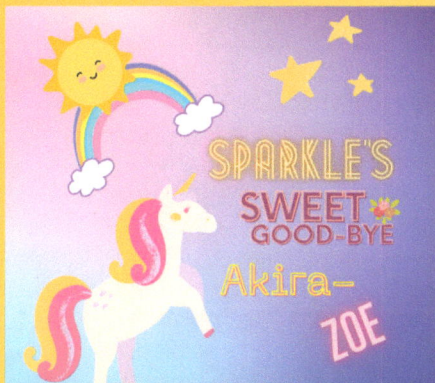

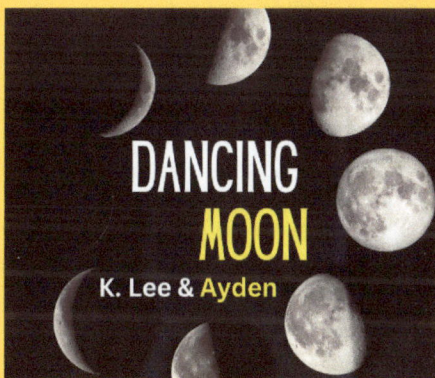

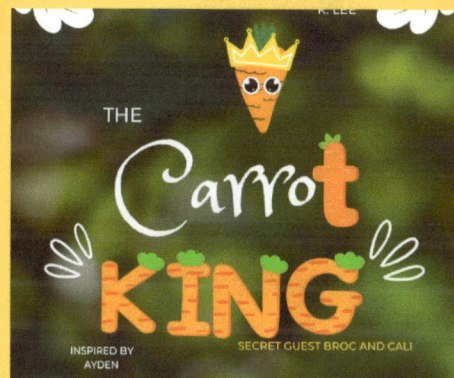

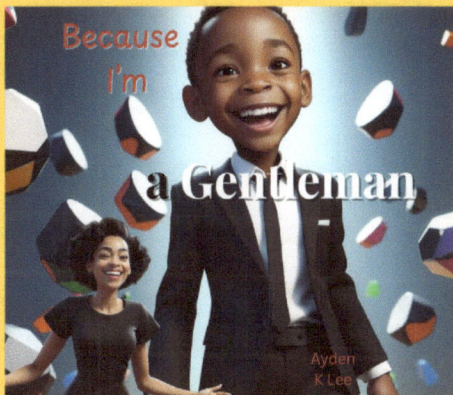

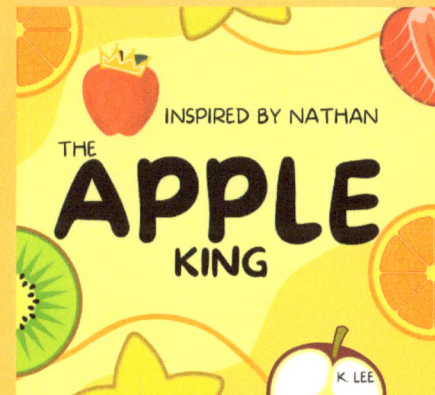

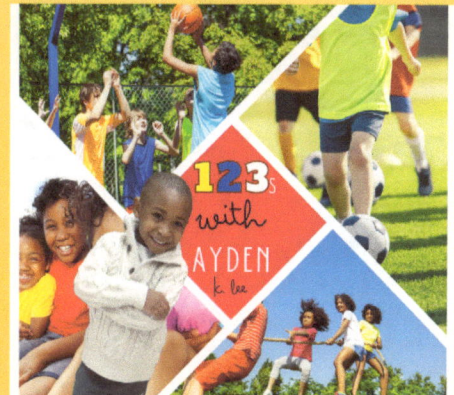

ARE YOU

sleepy, Baby!

K. Lee

SPARKLE'S
SWEET
GOOD-BYE
Akira-
ZOE

ABCs
WITH NATHAN

K. LEE

YUCK or YUM

DANCING
MOON
K. Lee & Ayden

THE
Carrot
KING
INSPIRED BY AYDEN
SECRET GUEST BROC AND CALI

K. LEE

Because I'm
a Gentleman
Ayden
K Lee

INSPIRED BY NATHAN
THE
APPLE
KING
K. LEE

123s
with
AYDEN
k. lee

Order More Books Today!

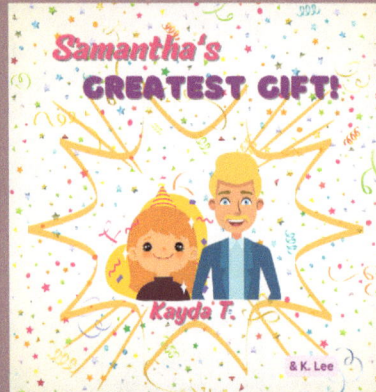

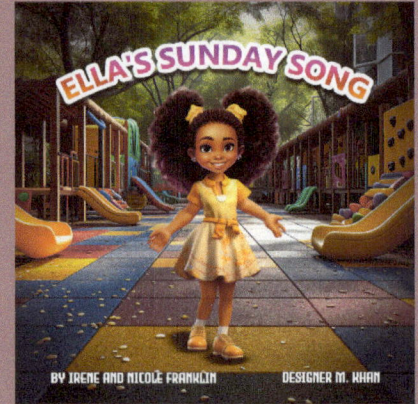

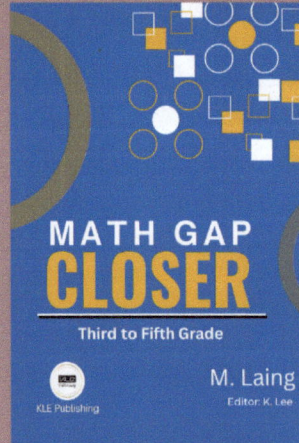